Giraffes

Giraffes

Jenny Markert

T H E   C H I L D ' S   W O R L D®, INC.

Published in the United States of America by The Child's World®, Inc.
PO Box 326
Chanhassen, MN 55317-0326
800-599-READ
www.childsworld.com

Product Manager Mary Berendes
Editor Katherine Stevenson
Designer Mary Berendes
Contributor Bob Temple

Photo Credits
ANIMALS ANIMALS © A. & M. Shah: 24
ANIMALS ANIMALS © Norbert Rosing: 20
© 2001 Art Wolfe/Stone: 29
© 1995 Craig Brandt: 13
© Daniel J. Cox/naturalexposures.com: 16
© 2001 Johan Elzenga/Stone: 23
© 1994 Kevin Schafer: 9
© 1998 Kevin Schafer: 19
© 1994 Mark J. Thomas/Dembinsky Photo Assoc. Inc.: cover
© Mary Ann McDonald/www.hoothollow.com: 2
© 1995 Robin Brandt: 15
© 1992 Stan Osolinski/Dembinsky Photo Assoc. Inc.: 10
© 1997 Stan Osolinski/Dembinsky Photo Assoc. Inc.: 6
© 2000 Stan Osolinski/Dembinsky Photo Assoc. Inc.: 30
© 2001 Renee Lynn/Stone: 26

Library of Congress Cataloging-in-Publication Data
Markert, Jenny.
Giraffes / by Jenny Markert.
p. cm.
Includes index.
ISBN 1-56766-879-8 (library bound : alk. paper)
1. Giraffe—Juvenile literature. [1. Giraffe.] I. Title.
QL737.U56 M37 2001
599.638—dc21
00-010783

On the cover...

Front cover: This reticulated giraffe lives in Kenya.
Page 2: This reticulated giraffe can curve its neck all the way around to scratch behind its leg.

Table of Contents

The grasslands are quiet under the hot African sun. A group of lions lies sleeping in the shade of a tree. In the distance, a tall, gangly animal walks slowly along. Its legs are long, its neck is even longer, and it is covered with big spots. It walks up to a tree and stretches its neck to bite leaves from a high branch. What is this strange creature? It's a giraffe!

⇐ This baringo giraffe is peeling the bark from a tree in Kenya.

What Are Giraffes?

Giraffes belong to a large group of animals called **mammals.** Mammals have hair and feed their babies milk from their bodies. Lions, monkeys, and people are mammals, too.

Giraffes are also **ruminants,** just like cows, sheep, and camels. Ruminants are animals that have stomachs with more than one part. When a ruminant eats, the food it swallows goes into the first part of its stomach. A little later, the animal burps up the food and rechews it. This rechewed food is called **cud.** When the animal has chewed the cud enough, it swallows it again. Then the cud moves on to the other parts of the stomach.

You can see this Masai giraffe's cheek puff out as it chews its cud. ⇒

What Do Giraffes Look Like?

Giraffes live in Africa, on huge plains of grass called **savannas.** Giraffes tower over all the other animals on the savanna. In fact, they're the tallest animals on land. They grow up to 17 feet tall, taller than a big playground slide!

Everything about a giraffe is long and slender. Even its tongue is long—up to 20 inches! An adult giraffe's legs are about as tall as a basketball player, and its neck is even longer. Despite its length, a giraffe's neck has only seven bones. You have the same number of bones in your neck.

⟸ It is easy to see this reticulated giraffe's body when it stands out in the open.

Are There Different Kinds of Giraffes?

There are nine different kinds of giraffes. Each has its own pattern of spots. *Reticulated giraffes* are the most famous type. You can often see them in pictures and books. Their spots look like a white and brown net. *Masai giraffes* are less well known and have leaf-shaped spots. *Baringo giraffes* (also called *Rothschild's giraffes*) have deep brown spots that are sometimes shaped like rectangles. *Nigerian giraffes* have pale, reddish yellow spots. *Cape giraffes* have rounded spots all the way down to their feet.

This male baringo giraffe has very dark spots. ⇒

The large lumps on a giraffe's head are bony horns covered with skin and hair. Most giraffes have only two horns, but some have three, four, or even five. At birth, a giraffe's horns are only about as long as your big toe. When the giraffe is fully grown, its horns can be longer than your foot.

It's easy to tell whether a giraffe is a male (called a **bull**) or a female (called a **cow**) by looking at its horns. Bulls have longer horns than cows. In addition, the hair covering a bull's horns is usually worn off. That's because the males use their horns when they fight with each other.

Can you tell whether these baringo giraffes are male or female? ⇒

Wild giraffes share the African savanna with animals such as antelopes, zebras, and wildebeests. These other animals compete for grasses and leaves that grow close to the ground. Giraffes, however, have a limitless supply of food. They eat the leaves in high trees that none of the other animals can reach.

They especially like to munch on *acacia* (uh-KAY-shuh) trees. Because giraffes are so large, they spend almost all of their time eating—sometimes up to 20 hours a day!

⇐ This baringo giraffe is nibbling on some high branches of an acacia tree.

How Do Giraffes Stay Safe?

Whenever giraffes eat, they keep a watchful eye on their surroundings. Lions sometimes try to sneak up on giraffes, but the giraffes can almost always see them coming. Giraffes have keen eyesight, and their height acts like a lookout tower. In fact, zebras and antelopes often stay near giraffes because the giraffes are so good at spotting danger.

If a lion comes too close, the giraffes take off running. Despite their height, they are graceful, fast runners. With their huge strides, they seem to float across the savanna. An adult giraffe can run about 35 miles per hour, though only for short distances.

This Masai giraffe is running from danger in Tanzania. ⇒

Being tall has many benefits, but it causes problems, too. Giraffes can't just flop down and rest whenever they are tired. It's quite a task for a long-legged giraffe to lower itself down to the ground—and quite a task to get back up again! Giraffes sit or lie down only when there are no enemies nearby. They usually sleep standing up.

⇐ This Masai giraffe has decided it is safe enough to lie down.

Giraffes must also be careful when they drink water. To reach the water, they must spread their front legs and sometimes bend their knees. In that position, they can't see enemies coming, and they can't defend themselves.

Luckily, giraffes don't have to drink water very often. The leaves they eat contain enough moisture to satisfy their thirst. In fact, giraffes usually avoid water. They prefer to walk around a water hole rather than through it—even if it's only ankle deep.

This Cape giraffe is drinking from a water hole in Zimbabwe. ⇒

Giraffes live in groups called **herds.** Most giraffe herds have between 10 and 20 animals. The herds are like big families. The herds' members (mostly females and babies) usually get along well with each other. They eat, rest, and play together. The older females take care of the young giraffes. The members of the herd also protect one another from enemies.

⇐ This herd of Masai giraffes is eating leaves off the same tree in Kenya.

Male giraffes fight with one another to be the leader of a herd. When they fight, two males stand side by side and swing their necks at each other. Each giraffe tries to poke its horns into the other giraffe's neck. The pokes hurt, but they don't injure the giraffes. The male who wins this test of strength gets to be the herd's leader.

← These male baringo giraffes are fighting with their horns.

What Are Baby Giraffes Like?

Baby giraffes come into the world with quite a bang. A female giraffe gives birth while standing up—so the newborn falls at least six feet to the ground! Although this is quite a fall, the baby, called a **calf,** rarely gets hurt.

Minutes after it is born, the calf can already stand on its long, shaky legs. It must stand so it can eat. At first the calf drinks only its mother's milk. When it is only three weeks old, it is already tall enough to eat the leaves on small trees. Still, the baby drinks its mother's milk for as long as two years. By the time it is four years old, the giraffe is fully grown. In the wild, giraffes can live to be about 25 years old.

This mother Cape giraffe is caring for her baby in South Africa. ⇒

Perhaps someday you will be able to visit Africa and see giraffes in the wild. As they graze on treetop leaves or amble across the open fields, giraffes are certainly the skyscrapers of the African plains!

← This female Cape giraffe lives in Kruger National Park in South Africa.

31

Glossary

bull (BULL)
A male giraffe is called a bull. Bull giraffes are larger than female giraffes.

calf (KAFF)
A baby giraffe is called a calf. Giraffe calves can stand up when they are only a few minutes old.

cow (KOW)
Female giraffes are called cows. Giraffe cows give birth to one baby at a time.

cud (KUD)
Cud is food that ruminants burp up and rechew. Giraffes chew cud.

herds (HERDZ)
Herds are groups of animals that live together. Giraffes live in herds of 10 to 20 animals.

mammals (MAM-mullz)
Mammals are animals that have hair or fur and feed their babies milk from their bodies. Giraffes are mammals, and so are people.

ruminants (ROO-mih-nents)
Ruminants are animals that have more than one part to their stomach and chew cud. Giraffes are ruminants.

savannas (suh-VAN-nuhs)
Savannas are hot, dry grasslands with a few trees and shrubs. Giraffes live on the African savannas.

Index

Web Sites

http://www.seaworld.org/animal_bytes/giraffeab.html

http://www.robinsonresearch.com/ANIMALS/MAMMALS/Artiodac/giraffe.htm

http://www.cmzoo.org/griaffeinfo.html

http://animaldiversity.ummz.umich.edu/accounts/giraffa/g._camelopardalis$narrative.html#geographic_range